1 MONTH OF FREE READING

at

www.ForgottenBooks.com

By purchasing this book you are eligible for one month membership to ForgottenBooks.com, giving you unlimited access to our entire collection of over 1,000,000 titles via our web site and mobile apps.

To claim your free month visit: www.forgottenbooks.com/free892773

ISBN 978-0-266-80926-5
PIBN 10892773

Historic, Archive Document

Do not assume content reflects current
scientific knowledge, policies, or practices.

Eufaula Pecan Company

Eufaula, Alabama

Partial view of our 75 acre Pecan Orchard, six years old. Many of these trees bearing. Young Cotton growing between trees.

ENTRANCE TO ORCHARD AND NURSERY.

CLIFF A. LOCKE   W. LAWRENCE WILD   CHARLES O. LOCKE

OWNERS

EUFAULA PECAN COMPANY

Eufaula, Alabama

Have several thousand budded and grafted pecan trees of the best varieties for delivery the coming Fall and Winter.

We extend a cordial invitation to prospective buyers to visit our Orchard and Nursery, of 75 acres located near the City limits.

Catalogue and prices mailed on application. Orders left with either member of the Company will have prompt attention.

Our trees are not handled by tree brokers and we have no agents.

EUFAULA PECAN CO.

PECANS.

For the past few years a great deal of attention has been given to the study of Pecans. Many have become interested in the growth of them, and thousands of acres have been set in commercial orchards, of the thin shell varieties of budded and grafted trees, throughout the Southern States. This is due largely to the fact that the Pecan is a very hardy and profitable tree, and adapts itself to varying conditions, and can be planted in various kinds of soil. The Pecan tree thrives best on rich, alluvial soil, but can be successfully grown on any well drained soil suitable for corn or cotton.

CARE OF TREES WHEN RECEIVED FROM NURSERY.

When trees are received from a nursery they may be kept for some time before planting, by digging a trench and covering the roots firmly with moist soil. When they are taken to the field to transplant, a wet sack should be put around them. The holes for trees should be amply large, about three feet deep and three feet wide, and the trees should be set as deep in the ground as they stood in the nursery from which they came. If they are transplanted in dry weather, a bucket or two of water should be poured into the hole, after the top soil has been thrown in about the roots. A shovel full or two of stable manure or one or two pounds of Commercial Fertilizer will be beneficial, if not placed too close to the roots. Before planting, all broken roots should be trimmed off. It has been said that if the tap root is cut the tree will not bear. This, however, is a mistake. But care should be taken not to cut off too much of it. We have numbers of bearing trees, the tap roots of which were cut back to about three feet. In setting trees five to eight feet, we always cut back the tops and leave about four to six feet above the ground.

WHEN TO PLANT.

Trees should be set from November 1st to the latter part of March, but trees planted late in the Spring need a great deal of additional care, such as watering, etc. The best months for planting are November, December and January, but taking all things into consideration, December is preferable, thus giving ample time for the winter rains to settle the dirt firmly about the roots of the trees.

. We are planting our orchard trees 45 x 45 feet, which we consider about the proper distance. Our first planting was 30 x 40 feet, which we now find, was entirely too close.

CULTIVATION.

It is well to grow a crop between the trees, especially before they begin bearing, such as peas, peanuts, melons, cotton, etc. The peas are especially good for this purpose. After the peas have been gathered, the vines can be turned under, thus fertilizing the soil. Around the young trees there should be left a space of from three to six feet, and more, as the trees grow older. This space should be kept free from grass and weeds.

AGE OF BEARING.

The age at which trees begin bearing is a much discussed question. Some few trees come into bearing at three years, a good many at five, and practically all between six and eight years. Of course trees fertilized and given especial care will bear earlier than those that are neglected. A tree that bears a full crop one year may be expected to have a smaller one the next year. Trees should begin to pay profitably at from eight to ten years, if they have been properly cared for, but do not expect to get the best results if the orchard has been neglected.

We are propagating the following varieties, all of which are fruiting in our orchards, and have proven very satisfactory.

We extend all prospective buyers a cordial invitation to visit us and see for themselves the result of our manner of cultivation.

There are many varieties of trees. Some are best adapted to one section, some to another. It is really better to have an orchard set with several varieties, as one variety will probably bear better one year, and another the next.

VAN DEMAN.

The original tree of this variety was grown from a nut planted in Union, St. James Parish, La., in 1836.

Description.

Size, large to very large; 50 to 60 nuts to the pound; long sharp base, and sharp apex; color, reddish brown; shell, moderately thin; kernel, long and plump; flavor, delicate, rich.

The tree is of strong, fairly erect habit, and is a moderately good bearer.

PABST.

The original tree is at Ocean Springs, Miss. It proved to be a specially good grower, yielding nuts of large size, and plump kernel, and was first propagated in 1890.

Description.

Size, large, averaging 50 to 55 nuts to the pound; form, short, cylindrical, with a very blunt, broadly grooved apex; shell, thick and hard; kernel, smooth and plump.

The Pabst is a sturdy, upright tree. It is fairly productive.

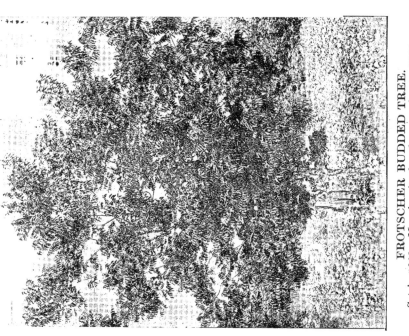

FROTSCHER BUDDED TREE.

Set in 1908. Now has its fourth crop of nuts, 1914.

STUART.

The original Stuart tree was in Pascagoula, Miss. It is supposed to have been grown from a nut brought from Mobile, Ala., and planted about 1874. Its average yield from 1889 to 1892 was 140 pounds per annum. In 1892 it yielded about 350 pounds.

Description.

Size, large to very large, about 50 or 55 nuts to the pound; rather long, with blunt apex, and rounded base; brownish gray; shell, rather thin; kernel, smooth and plump; flavor, rich and delicate.

The Stuart tree is a strong, upright grower. It is proving regularly and abundantly productive in most localities where it has been fruited, and is apparently succeeding over a wider climatic range than any other variety thus far tested.

FROTSCHER.

This variety was originated at Olivier, Iberia Parish, La. It was planted about 1860.

Description.

Large size, averaging about 50 to 55 nuts to the pound. Form, cylindrical oval, with rounded base, and blunt apex; color, yellowish brown; flavor, pleasant.

The Frotscher is a vigorous grower of spreading habit, and with us is proving a very satisfactory variety.

GROWING SWEET AND IRISH POTATOES IN YOUNG ORCHARD.

SUCCESS.

inal tree is at Ocean Springs, Miss., where it was grown from a nut, sup-
been planted in 1890.

Description.

ge, running about 50 to 55 nuts to the pound. Shape, oblong, with sharply
d blunt apex; shell, of medium thickness; kernel, plump, bright, and of
and of a very good quality.
is a vigorous and rather upright grower, and with us is proving regularly

SCHLEY.

iety is supposed to be a seedling of a Stuart, planted about 1881.

Description.

:dium to large, ranging from 60 to 65 nuts to the pound. Oblong, with coni-
. very thin; kernel, long, slender, bright; flavor, delicate, sweet, and rich.
e is a rather slender, upright grower, and with us has not been a very heavy
consider it one of the best varieties.

YOUNG ORCHARD JUST PLANTE *D* IN PEAS.

DELMAS.

The original tree was grown from a nut planted at Scranton, Miss., about 1877. It began bearing in 1884.

Description.

Size, large to very large; 50 to 55 nuts to the pound; form, oblong ovate, pointed at base, and blunt at apex; shell, rather thick; kernel, plump and well filled; bright straw color, very attractive; flavor, sweet and pleasant.

The Delmas tree is a strong grower, of erect and roundish head. It is productive and promising.

PABST TREE,
Set in 1908. Bearing, 1914, Second Crop.

PRICE OF PECAN TREES.

1	10	100
$ .50	$ 4.50	$ 40.00
.55	5.00	45.00
.65	6.00	55.00
.75	6.50	65.00
$1.00	9.00	80.00
1.25	10.00	90.00
2.00	15.00	125.00

es go at 10 rates, 50 at 100 rates, etc.

he had top-grafted in 1907, with Stuart and Success grafts. The trees then being 13 year old seedlings. Six years later (1913) he realized from his crop of nuts 8 per cent. on a valuation of $750.00 per acre.